"*Morning Night* is an inspiring collection of soul-filling and spirit-enlivening poetry. Rooted and soaring, inviting us inward and outward to see and experience life's fullness. Larry's words evocatively capture the breadth and depth of being human in this beautiful, broken world. Take a deep breath. Savor each poem. Return to them again and again."

—**Reverend Dr. Beth Johnson,** Unitarian Universalist minister

"Larry Ward generously offers us deep teachings and powerful insights on love, grief, anger, tenderness, compassion, and inter-connection based on his lifetime of engaged mindfulness prac-tice. Each poem is a delicious and unique gem. This book is a companion to turn to in moments of crisis and joy for guidance and inspiration. Any time you open this book, you will always find something new. This book is a true gift."

—**Elli Weisbaum, PhD,** Assistant Professor, Buddhism, Psychology & Mental Health program (BPMH), Faculty of Arts and Sciences, Department of Psychiatry, Temerty Faculty of Medicine

"I was surprised and moved both times I read *Morning Night*. Minding the meditative gaps between his breaths, recognizing the reality of interbeing and interdependence with the more than human world, observing the ways profound ignorance distorts loving bliss, like a bell breaking through our slumber, poet Larry Ward invites us into his artful expressions of awakening. Wake up! Wake up!"

—**Pamela Ayo Yetunde,** author of *Dearly Beloved: Prince, Spirituality, and This Thing Called Life*

"Larry Ward's poetry falls on us like rain, refreshing, renewing, leading us through darkness to light, returning us to the begin-ning in the center of the heart."

—**Dr. Ava Avalos,** dancer and Dharma teacher, Botswana

"There is a wisdom that lives beyond the confines of rational thought—one that can only be expressed in poems and songs. In *Morning Night*, Larry Ward offers that kind of wisdom. These poems are for our times: illuminating both pain and possibility, offering sanctuary, and guiding us back to the deep belonging we share with each other, spirt, and earth. This book is not just to be read—it is to be felt, breathed, and remembered."

—**Kazu Haga,** author of *Fierce Vulnerability*

"Reading the profound poems of Larry Ward, you will find yourself immersed in the holy dharma of suffering, awakenment, wisdom, and compassion. Again and again, you encounter the absolute and the relative, and feel the love of mother, sibling, grandmother, friend, teacher, and spouse. You experience sorrow, fear, and tragedy, and delight in deer, caterpillars, birds, trees, and rain. Enlightenment, hail!"

—**Robertson Work,** nonfiction author, social activist, and former UNDP policy advisor and NYU Wagner professor

"Larry Ward's teachings are based on his own authentic transformative experience of being a Black man who also holds a high and honored Dharma seat in the lineage of Thich Nhat Hanh."

—**Zenju Earthlyn Manuel,** poet, author, ordained Zen priest, and medicine woman of the Drum

"*Morning Night* is a brilliant assemblage of poetic wisdom: an embrace for the soul. Perfectly aligned with the sacred texts of diverse spiritual traditions that offer wisdom through parable, story, and verse, Dr. Ward delivers dharma and divine wisdom from many lineages in odes to life itself. Get this modern masterpiece today and prepare for utter delight."

—**Dr. Kamilah Majied,** author of *Joyfully Just*

PRAISE FOR *MORNING NIGHT*

"These poems are soulful music from the wisdom of the heart. They invite and welcome us into deep insight and vast compassionate love for all beings. We are strengthened and empowered by these blessings from the ancestors."

—**Gaylon Ferguson, PhD,** author of *Welcoming Beginner's Mind*

"*Morning Night* is a luminous offering from the heart of a devoted practitioner, poet, and global elder. These poems speak plainly to the wounds of this world—violence, racism, loss—and still shimmer with the moonlight of a heart that remains untouched, free, and full of love. His words bear the imprint of a lifetime walking the path with humility and insight.

Larry offers not just poetry, but refuge. These are poems to sit with in silence, to return to in struggle, and to lean into when we need to remember what is still possible. This is the dharma sung through a poet's heart—tender, unflinching, and full of the strength of stillness. We need this voice now. We need this book now."

—**Kaira Jewel Lingo**, Buddhist teacher, author of *We Were Made for These Times,* co-author of *Healing Our Way Home*

"A selfless teacher for over 30 years, Dr. Larry Ward offers his brilliance through the lens of a life in the Dharma on the plight of the world, sharing nuggets of insight on how we can save it and ourselves."

—**Sister Peace,** Buddhist nun, Plum Village tradition

"*Morning Night* is evidence of a seasoned teacher looking deeply, documenting insights from lessons learned and illuminations to ponder forward. Each heartfelt inquiry a reflection on personal, social, and spiritual relationship in this present moment, serving as a mirror to help us as readers contemplate our connection with life indefinitely. This is a wonderful poetry collection."

—**Brett Cook,** interdisciplinary artist

"Larry Ward is a great soul."

—**Jean Houston, PhD,** author, scholar, and philosopher

"Larry Ward's poetry evokes timeless attention to the deepest mysteries of life and calls us to attune to our body's rhythms even as we contend with pressure and chaos in our lives. He compels us to notice the simple things—sounds, the weave of a spider's web, our breath—to bring forth a quietness that can often feel elusive in the midst of racial violence and despair. Ward is telling us: The busy tasks and heartbreak that consume your mind are not all there is. Go deeper. Rest. Behold."

—**Rima Vesely-Flad, PhD,** author of *Black Buddhists and the Black Radical Tradition*

"Dr. Larry Ward is an elder in American Buddhism, using his decades of heart-centered practice to guide our community into a deeper and more relevant exploration of America's struggle with racism. We will all be much freer because of Dr. Ward's teaching."

—**Lama Rod Owens,** author of *Love and Rage, Radical Dharma,* and *The New Saints*

"Grounded in mindful presence, the wisdom of lived experience, and an undefended heart, beloved Plum Village Dharma teacher Larry Ward's poetry shines with luminosity and clarity. Each page a calming presence and a gift of peacemaking, a legacy of love. Ward's poetry, more a prayer, offers guidance and grace born from his decades-long mindfulness practice as a student of Zen master Thich Nhat Hanh. This is a book to savor slowly."

—**Valerie Brown,** Quaker, Dharma teacher, and author of *Hope Leans Forward*

MORNING
NIGHT

MORNING NIGHT

POEMS ON SPIRIT, RACE AND NATURE

LARRY WARD, PhD

Lotus Moss
PRESS

Lotus Moss Press

For more information or to contact the author, visit www.thelotusinstitute.org.

Illustrations: Larry Ward
Design and project management: Elizabeth Chambers
Publishing consultant: Martha Bullen
Copyeditor: Erik Fuhrer, Yellow Bird Editors
Author photo: Kate Cumming

ISBN: 979-8-9992475-3-7 (paperback)
ISBN: 979-8-9992475-2-0 (ebook)
ISBN: 979-8-9992475-4-4 (hardcover)

Reprinted with permission from *Love's Garden*, 2008, published by Parallax Press: "I have been Hurt by Falling Dreams" and "Larry's Love Letter to the World".

Reprinted with permission from *America's Racial Karma*, 2020, published by Parallax Press: "When I Became Currency" and "Somebody Stole my Face".

Library of Congress Control Number: 2025916952

Printed in the United States of America

*To Peggy Rowe, my wife, my love, and my partner
in the Dharma Way. She serves as the first reader
of everything I write and has always encouraged me
to bring my poetry into the world.
I am immensely thankful and honored by her unfailing
encouragement and continuous support.
She is the superpower that lifts up my words,
for which I am humbled and grateful.*

Larry Ward, untitled, mixed media, 2022.

CONTENTS

Race: Clouds Over the Moon

Nature: Light in the Forest

INTRODUCTION

My first memories of poetry are from Bible study groups.
There's some great poetry in the Old and New Testaments.
Similarly, Negro spirituals are alive with rhythm and dance.
I started singing in a gospel choir at an early age. I remember my first encounter with the poet Langston Hughes,
who was a high school graduate from my hometown of
Cleveland, Ohio. In junior high, *Beowulf,* alongside works
by Chaucer and Shakespeare, intrigued and captivated
me. These works stimulated my imagination and poetic
expression.

Tales of Paul Laurence Dunbar and the prose and poetry
of Phillis Wheatley filled the air of Cleveland's East Side.
Wheatley, the first published African American poet,
was from my neighborhood. She offered me hope and
possibility. On the verge of publishing my first poetry
collection, I feel like I am at the tailor getting fitted for my
graduation suit. Or maybe I am a baby bird being pushed
out of the nest and into the wide blue sky. I never thought
of myself as a poet. I simply made a note whenever I
was visited by a poem. These visitations happen more
frequently when I am attending or facilitating a silent
retreat. I have become accustomed to reading these poems
in these sacred spaces. Peggy, Grace, Karen, and Liz helped
me to collect them, and I humbly offer them to you.

Each poem in this collection is a guest that arrived with
a flashlight at the cave of my heart. Please join me on
the wonderful adventure of exploring these interior and
exterior landscapes. May each poem bring warmth and
light into the cave of your own heart.

The collection is divided into three sections, as follows:

Spirit: Finding My Way Home

This first section illuminates the importance of a spiritual life of practice that cultivates insight into our non-separation and warmth of compassion for all beings. The theme of spirit cultivates a sense of mindfulness toward lived experience, creating a path to wholesome happiness, self-transformation, and social justice.

Race: Clouds Over the Moon

These poems rise from my awareness of my historical racial position. They explore how the fabrication of race as the essence of identity has perfumed our social fabric and had a systemic impact on daily life. For me, our shared humanity is often lost in the social impact of racialized consciousness.

Nature: Light in the Forest

This section explores intimate experiences with the natural world of which we are all an integral part. The natural world provides a mirror for the mysterious human experiences of living, aging, and dying. These poems reflect an experience of non-duality, illuminating the shared nature of what appears both inside and outside of us, and celebrating our connection with nature.

Larry Ward, untitled, water color, pen and ink, 2022.

SPIRIT
Finding My Way Home

Sit With Me

Where are you running
to my friend with
your mind dizzy
with the things of the world
and your stomach bloated
from too much?

Please stop, come home,
sit with me in
the cool night air
listen to the sound
of the garden trees
in the silence of the night.

See the miracle of
the spider web in
front of your face
with its luminous lines
connecting heaven and
Earth. Relax and enjoy
your breathing.

One day everything we
see, touch, feel, and imagine
will all disappear.
Smile while you
are in the here and
now.

Let all of your worries
and fears float
down the river
of tears. No need to cling.
Fluttering in the wind as
prayer flags.

Aging at the Well

I am shocked at the well,
my hands no longer grip the pump as firmly.
I'm not as strong as I used to be.

I can hear the water coming.
Slowly and carefully, I receive it with grace.

Every now and then I touch the realm of no fear.
Pain in my legs brings me back to life.

Our little life is big:
millions of ancestors, all marks of evolution.

Hanging around for a while
lifted up by love.

Feeling my body waning,
vanishing and appearing every moment.

Ancestors pushing me forward
into stages of my precious life.
Aging's grace and peace reside in me.

I Bow

I saw compassion appear
in the hillsides and valleys of this world.
Beloved community
climbing hope's holy mountain.

Sitting under an emerald buddha
in a cave of light
called me back to my breath.

I remembered my death.
Life's mystery dancing
before my eyes.

Heart remembers
above and below.
Sounds of angel's whispers.
I bow.

A Poem for Sandra

Rest your breath, rest your body,
rest your mind, and rest your
heart in this holy moment.

Out of my window I see
the leaves falling: gold, red
brown and brilliant yellow.

Falling into death and birth
again and again.
Falling into Paradise.

Sister moon vanishes from our small view,
yet, she forever remains in the
symphony of vast time and space.

My dearest Sandra, the sun
still shines on your face.
Even the face you had before
you were born. No harm
can come to such a face.

Even leaves fall in paradise.
Don't worry, my dear one.
You are in paradise to stay.

Rest your breath, rest your body,
rest your mind, and rest your
heart in this holy moment.

A Vow

A vow is like the
wind at your back,
like the path
to the ocean above
the sangha shore.

A full and open heart
of just one person
is enough
to change the world.

The full and open heart
of two people can cause
the sun and moon to move
and the stars to shine
brighter than ever.

Growth

Even in darkest night
red lotuses.
Under shadows a still pond
awaiting morning light.

Eyes of moonlight
dancing, merging
over millions of years:
What's your hurry?

Noble silence of deep
space, unlimited
comfort in its holy arms.
Suffering as companion.

A Perfume River Boat Ride

Around the bend of the Perfume River
our dragon boat took time.
Above steep ancient stone steps
stood a golden pagoda constructed by an emperor
silently resting on the earth,
its seven levels reaching for the sky.

Surprised with its simplicity, grace, and beauty,
the grounds, the temple, the sound of the bell
still echoes in my heart,

touching the earth three times:
In touch with my breath.
In touch with my heart.
In touch with my devotion.

Here Bonsai trees laugh at my notions of age.
Surrounded by living graves of ancestors,
ancient temple, and pine trees.

Thousands gathered for a day with Thay.
A striking view of Hue.
A red tea house peaks through jackfruit trees,
a gentle smiling monk revealed.

I made this pilgrimage three times.
Who knew
I would be so moved
by quiet love?

Old Blue Austin

Thich Quang Duc rode in an old blue Austin
that day in Saigon, 1963:
a vehicle for offering his life.
Engulfed in flames, perfect peace.

Lotus in a sea of fire.
Compassion speaks to end war now.

Temple Sounds

Listen to the sound
of the big temple
bell echoing
in the night.

Hear the young monk
chanting prayers and blessings
and know where
and who you are.

When the time comes,
you will know
the time has come.
Touch the earth
and rejoice.

Dear Kyoto

I.
Dear Kyoto, I have
searched for you and
you have found me.

II.
Maple leaves are turning
red. I make a deep bow
to the abbot.

A gift of a new robe.
Maybe it's time to wander
no more.

III.
My Kyoto,
train tracks of time.
Feeling surprised.
Feeling at home.

IV.
Footsteps on ancient
pathways. Temples
and shrines at every turn.
Fleeting moments.
Happiness tears too.

V.
Rivers of my heart
flowing freely.
The way of beauty remembered.

Rain drops
on my umbrella,
I wake up.
Magic again.

Untouched

This world keeps breaking
my heart. Under a blanket of
stars I meet my own restlessness
and doubt.

My footsteps touch stardust
at every moment.
Moonlight continues to shine.

In a quiet moment of love,
I realize that my pure
heart and pure mind, like
the moon, remains untouched.

Experiences of violence,
hate, loss, and discrimination
have not harmed me.

Dear friend, stay in touch
with your mind
of love, whispers the owl.

Now my only wish is that I
can live a life that is
a prayer, that encourages
more love in this world.

Enter Your Life

Enter your life
like an epic poem. Ride
the colors of change
with the wind unattached.

In light of the coming
and going of all things, savor
the stars in the dark blue sky, trust
the sun in your heart to guide you home.

Here between earth and sky, listen!
Hear your footsteps in the leaves of time.
Fix your gaze on the horizon of not yet but.
Stay in this moment and ask
in this great symphony,

What is my instrument? What is my music?
What is my song?

Surrender to this crucible's alchemy
as it creates the mandala of your holy life.

Cross the lake of life's mystery
as a fearless swan, embodying grace,
peace, and compassion as you
head toward the distant shore.

My Teacher, My Breath

Because of you, my feet
are planted on higher ground.
The sun in my heart still shines.

Even though I walk through
the waves of birth and death
caused by the conditions of this
world, I remain fearless.
My path is clear.

I surrender. I lay down
my burden of pain by
the riverside. I wake up
each day hoping the world
won't break my heart. But it does,
again, and again.
Break it open, I say.

I call on you to help me
not be fallen at the flood
carried away in flows of
fear, anger, and regret.

May the holy ground of forgiveness
catch me when I fall
from the ubiquitous grace that
like the moonlight,
in the darkest of night,
lights up my path.

My teacher, my breath,
keep me close to the heartbeat
of my precious life and
to my heart's call, ever
widening, until the pain
of all beings
I can recognize as my own.

Still in Love with Life

I have been hurt by dreams
tumbling down like great stones from
the mountain of hope, cracking open my heart.

Feeling like I am losing everything,
being ground up
by the world of endurance.

Tired, sad, and weary
my eyes overflowing with tears.
I find myself wrapped in clouds of doubt.

I was certain the moon stole my shoes.
I searched everywhere,
over the green countryside,

in crowded city streets,
brown deserts, the snow-capped mountains.
Even the dust of stars were empty.

Meeting fury, coursing
through pulsing veins, a silent illness
when life did not go my way.

In the softness of one holy night
the Dharma rain fell.

My head was wet with the tears of heaven.
The sky cleared.

I looked down
and discovered that my shoes
had been on my feet all along.

My pure heart and my pure mind
have not been crushed or destroyed
by disappointment and hatred.

My deepest desire
is to be a poem and live a prayer
that encourages more love in this world.

Moonlight of True Love

Maybe it has been a while since you've been to your garden.
Maybe it has been covered over with weeds
of pain, disappointment, or grief.
Maybe it has been hidden from sight by your busyness,
anxiety, or momentary excitement.

Even if it seems barren, its appearance, though real, is false.
Look, your garden is always full of seeds
waiting to be touched by love's moonlight,
revealing the beauty of the night sky.
Moonbeams caress tree-tops,
nourishing the earth with drops of dew.

Lighting our way in the dark,
the path of meditation opens my heart.
The invitation to love,
non-fear
kindness
compassion
joy and
equanimity
is present in this very moment.

This is the moonlight of true love.

Morning Night

In the morning night
I died for you.
Why do you look away from me?
Time is slow and fast.

Across the river,
I bathe in moonlight
with you, always
passing away and arriving.

Always now.
Always later.
I'll be at the river
in the morning night.

Mother's Hug

In the middle of this week,
I missed my mother so much.

I wished for a hug.
Awareness arose.

My heart; her heart. Touching
in the here and now.

Tender is the Heart

Tender is the heart
that sees the miracle
when the days of seeing oneself are over,
when feet no longer feel the earth
or the rain no longer falls on the head.

The song of nature has its own timing.
Mystery happens all day and all night.
Voices hum and flutter, sights come and go.

Interbeing, impermanence, and nirvana.
The bees come round at 11:30. It's warmer then.
Frogs gather at night emitting weird chants.
Crows ballet throughout the day.
The turkeys arrive walking slowly, looking around.

We are graced by the flight of the blue herons
catching the wind. We look up.
Tender is the heart that sees the miracle.

The Crossing

To cross the great water of frozen
perception is the great adventure
of our epoch.

Learning to love is the great path
of all earthlings, bound to
this world of disturbance and light.

Stepping out of the constructs
created by others to be
less than, more than, even equal.

We have been underestimated.
You can feel it in your heart.
We shape ourselves.

We are no longer caught in the net
of shiny things or
rusty ideas of power.

We shape ourselves
again and again,
tasting freedom and radiance.

The Journey Home

On the journey home
you may traverse mountains of doubt
and valleys of discontent.
Do not take them too seriously.

Just over the great water
a fresh breath.

Look my friend!
At the edge of your heartbreak
is your holy life,
ready to be lived like Francis.

Purple flowers of the jacaranda
fall from the sky with perfect timing.

The agapanthus' purple petals raise up
from the earth, reaching for light
like a harmonious symphony.

Covered with betrayal's red dust
your heart is caught in waves of uncertainty.

The horseshoe has turned the wrong way,
it seems your luck has vanished.

The bitter taste of loss is in your mouth.
Disoriented, you fall up the slopes of time.

Wake up, wake up, wake up, my friend.
Your heart is looking for you.

Larry Ward, untitled, mixed media, 2022. Upper left section of painting used on the cover.

What Can I Say About My Beloved Teacher?

I can say
that the whisper of his voice
in the dark night of confusion,
fear, and sorrow,
calls us home to our true selves.

I can say
that his teachings
bring the dharma rain,
bathing us in healing energy,
in the blessed peace of our lives.

I can say
that his gentle footsteps
ride on the winds of peace,
the thunder of compassion,
and reflect the moonlight
of understanding.

I can say
that he tirelessly engages
with his whole being
in the noblest of causes,
to heal and transform
the breaking waves of our shadows.

I can say
I love my teacher
because he has nourished
the teacher in me to wake up,
wake up, wake up.

I can say
that his practice, his prose,
and his poetry speaks
with the beauty
and clarity of the Buddha
within each of us.

I can say
that on this very day we
are most fortunate
to be here together,
to be in touch with
the miracle of deep breath
and the holy moment of awareness
in which we are touched
by that which is not coming and not going.

Here we are together in the heart
of Thich Nhat Hanh.

The Lamp

The most beautiful lamp I ever saw
was made from pieces of glass
left on the floor at the end of the day
in the artist's workshop.

The pieces sparkled, hidden
until seen as a dance of colors and light.
With tender care, a full heart's hands reconstructed it,
singing the brilliance of new wholeness.

Hey you, on this day, look down
at the floor of your life, your heart.
See the pieces of pain and joy lying
on the floor waiting for you.

Do not be disheartened. With tender care and patience
take these pieces with the hands of a full heart.
Take these pieces of your precious life and beauty make
for yourself and for all.

Whidbey Gathering

Into the circle of all beings we have come,
with the sunshine, tree, raven, coyote, deer,
rabbit, stars and precious moonlight.

Beloved Community is our hearts greatest desire,
our human birthright,
our destiny in every moment.
It lives in our bones and minds as a dream deferred.

Yet here we are, now, touching and touched by its true presence.
Celebrate this moment, this gathering of working dreams.
I join my hands and pray
that buddhas and bodhisattvas throughout space and time
rise up from the earth at this precious hour.

May these sacred energies bless us with boundless love
and awaken within us our very best selves.

May they sing the songs of those who have come
through the mists of ignorance.

May the cup of compassion within our hearts pour out
covering the earth, both near and far.

May our feet walk gently in the sands of time, echoing purpose,
peace, and creative caring throughout this green land.

May the nectar of kindness touch our lips as we speak.
May we find in ourselves the vast blue sky of inclusiveness.

May our hands turn the wheel of time
toward a more just and beautiful world,
a world worthy of our holy lives.

Rest in Beauty

Just the other day I saw driftwood
floating in Puget Sound
carried away by a deep current.
Where are you floating to my friend?
With your heart and mind busy
with the things of this world
and your stomach still empty
from too much.

Please stop. Come home,
sit with me in the cool morning air.
Listen to the sound of the ocean
and the silence.
See the miracle of the spider or the ant
or the star or the cloud or the moon,
in front of your face, luminous,
reflecting both heaven and earth.

Look, Listen

The companions of my suffering are
the gateway to my healing transformation,
not to be hated, feared or clung to,
but stirred wisely as ingredients into the
new soup of my precious life.

It is here now, always
the glorious sunlight, gentle morning breeze.
Forgiveness is the fabric of nature,
the river flows on, carrying the past but
letting it go at the same time.

Look, listen to the birdsong,
the frogs at the pond are dancing
in the moonlight and calling your name.
Your name, your name, echoing
across the starry night sky.

Seven

I have sat facing the wall to nowhere
for seven days,
seven years,
seven lifetimes,
in the thundering silence of my life.
Now I turn towards the water to recognize myself.
I walk in the dharma rain nourished by what comes.

Here I witness the large waves, the small waves,
and the tiny movements of life in the ocean.
I remember that I too am a wave.
I rise and fall as the ocean.
We are one at every moment.

I want to be touched and moved
by the wind in all directions,
to greet all creatures large and small,
so that I am not confused by the sunrise and the sunset
of this life on loan for a while
until I appear to vanish from your view.

Mother's Laugh

A puff of cloud,
grass trembling in the wind,
the grace of the blue sky.

The smile of the moonlight,
my mother's laugh
high, sparkling, heart-opening
goodness flowing through her bones
connecting mine to beginningless time.

Here, in the suchness of all things,
don't hold back your tears.
The desert of our hearts must be watered
for the flowers to bloom.

Way of Beauty

I am here now, walking on this precious red earth
the smile of the moonlight
the grace of the trees in wintertime.

I want to be awake when the stars come
to gather me up in their arms,
when the earth whispers goodbye for now.

I dwell in the sacred thus-ness
beyond words and beyond forms.

I walk through this world with love's wisdom
in my heart and deep justice in my mind.

My bones rejoice in the joy of beauty's way,
shining and blessing all in the ten directions.

Peace

May I be on even terms with all that exists and does not exist
in touch with the original breath for all my days.

May I be on even terms with the original breath as I walk
among that which exists and does not exist in every moment.

In this way I may realize the liberation of my heart and mind
as I attend the funeral of all my sorrows.

At home there is calm, still certainty. In peace I am undisturbed
by the coming and going of things great and small.

Ah, the breath of equanimity. In so being moved,
compassion, joy, loving-kindness are my companions.

Life after life.
Blessing the world.

I see. I see. I see.
The Buddha smiled.

The Promise

We engage through our love,
opening 10,000 dharma doors
with a true mind and a true heart.
What do we call this urgency?
It matters not.

The sun rises and the moon shines without confusion.
Listen to the frogs. Do they remind you of anyone?
The bamboo chimes dance in the wind without clinging.
Our chants sing out beauty
like the birds greeting the morning sun.

We are here to be engaged, to remember the promise
we made, many lifetimes ago
not to leave anyone behind,
not to ignore the suffering of any being,
to remember our noble calling.
It has not changed.
Wake up, wake up, wake up.

A Visit with Verna

In my sister's eyes
grief and gratitude mix
like potter's clay.

The end of things is so clear.
All arrogance is a waste,
all judgment incorrect.

The winds of time make all
outcomes temporary and
eternal.

Love Flows

I didn't know I was adopted,
until age seven.
I hid my sorrow under a moonrock.

I held hands with ancestors
of blood, land, and spirit.
They trembled with power. I saluted.

Love flowed into me.
Roy and Viola Ward, Miss Miller, Miss Fox,
Ollie and Marion Tindal
Whole churches, Pentecostal, Baptist and Lutheran.

Controlling nothing, trusting forever
in the blessings of love.
Here is my peace.
Years of love vibrate through my heart.

Dawn

White and red dogwood trees reach toward the blue sky.
Yellow daffodils shoot-up from the earth.
Bright forsythias sway in the gentle breeze.
The warmth of sunlight, the freshness of spring, is in me
opening, growing, smiling to life.

There is not much time left, the earth continues to turn.
I am certain now, what I must do
I am out of rhythm with the one who knows
I steal moments to come home to myself.
In the still of the night, I sing the songs of silence.

At the dawn, I find my breath in the morning mist.
Birds are singing, outside my window.
The sound of their wings flit over the pond.
It takes a lot of time to offer the best of myself.
I have not had it and it makes me sad.

A beam of moonlight has changed everything.
A ride on Perfume River brought me all the way home.
Floating candles drift away.
Please stay in the pagoda, says the abbott.
If only I could.

I am here now, waking up in the changing room
of my soul's department store.
I am becoming what my young self once knew.
Gazing at stars from the attic window,
I follow a yellow and green caterpillar on the sidewalk
to new worlds.

A Worthy Vow

In the lake of awakening,
I find calm.
My pure heart speaks.

I look to those first assembled
at the tree of awakening
dwelling on an island of mindfulness.

Witness lovingkindness
rising from the prayers of
untold compassionate hearts.

Circling earth,
blessing all ten directions with love,
emanating light.

The breath of all beings
finds ease.
What a noble calling.

Such a vow persists and flows
through birth and death,
beating the dharma drum,
from buddha field
to buddha field,
hidden in the hearts of all.

So Close to My Heart Am I

So close to my heart am I,
I can feel its gate swinging
with the touch of your love.

How could this be? It seems
like only yesterday when
we first met and said hello.

I bow to the emerald Buddha,
shining near and far, calling
me home. Yet here I remain

in love with the dharma light
shining from your eyes.

I am moved to tears
of openness, wishing for
our happiness.
Today we say goodbye.

Verses from Hell

1.
Hell is in my speech.
My speech is in my heart.
My heart is in me.
I am continuation.
My continuation rests in emptiness.

Hell is in my mood
in the beat of my thoughts.

Yet, I am more than this theater of mind-sense.

I feel trapped to myself.
I cannot seem to escape this torment.

No sense of home within myself.
No sense of safety, no sense of contentment.

I am on the river of outburst.
This sacred fury with injustice will not go away.

I whisper my pain to myself.
The mirror of my ego is cracked.

Light is seeping in.
I dance with my fury.

I see myself as victim,
perpetrator, and judge.

2.

The punisher lives in my mind, in the shadows
I start to remember. I start to feel the burning of hatred.

I start to feel the numbness of a frozen heart.
I realize I am in the metroplex of my mind,
in one of the seductive theaters.

I'm coming to rest now in the Buddha's mind.
As I reside in this space, the fire subsides.
Feeling returns to my heartbeat and energy to my limbs.

I am free as I have always been.
The hell realm is merely one movie of the mind.
The show is over for now.

This Sun

The sun rises over the mountains,
full of green,
full of life of many beings,
birds, ducks, turkeys, hawks, sparrows,
and hummingbirds.

This sun, this very sun
is in your heart as well.
In unlimited space and time,
it births many worlds.
It hides every day in the night
that we may come
accustomed to a singular grace.

In this miraculousness,
we may realize our own miraculousness.
Since we are the sun,
the morning,
the green,
the birds, hawk, trees, night, duck, turkey,
and sparrow.

Surrender

The birds are already enjoying their chorus.
The morning mist surrounds me in every direction.
Light shimmers off the branches of treetops reaching
for the sky.

Slowing down can make one a little anxious!

What insight,
what questions,
what emotions hidden
in the depths may rise
like a great dragon
from the ocean of my mind?

Whispering my name as it rises,
like the sun approaching ever so softly
but deliberately encompassing my direction,
reveals the landscape of my heart.

I surrender to the sun's majestic movement,
opening the day and night.
As the mist clears, I can see my way now
in the forest,
whether dark or light.

Celebration

The Calla lilies are beautiful.
Strong, exquisite, breathtaking.
They bloom only for a short time,
offering themselves to us. We are
like that too and that is enough.

The sun and moon were both
there on that great day,
as witness to the joining of two streams of
ancestors, what a wonder to behold!

What a joy to marry my wife, surrounded
by sangha, nourished by
the beautiful countryside of green
and early morning dew.

The Last Ride

When we take our animal
friend for the last ride
our hearts break open.

Dance of the Lightning Bugs

Under the blue night sky,
lightning bugs dance,
in the green valley.

They dance for a brief time,
offering freshness, delight, marvel.

Are they different
from the lightning bugs I saw yesterday?

Does it matter?
How would I know?
I stand amazed.

Maybe

I will write a poem maybe, if
my heart can catch one as it comes,
like a bird catches the wind.

Yesterday at 2:35
there was a large goose standing
on the deck right here at the lake's edge,
calling, talking, making sound.

A short distance away,
another goose in silence,
noticing, watching, standing
on the same deck listening.

I will write a poem maybe, if
my heart can catch one as it comes,
like a bird catches the wind.

Even in the darkest hour last night,
the Ponderosa Pines were caught
by the grace of the wind, to be shaped
and reshaped by the mysteries
of time and space, within
their sacred presence, sustained
in this little act of daring.

Sila's Shining Light

Those who have defined what is real and valuable
for centuries are now quaking in their shoes.

In the midst of this foray into our hearts and minds,
pointing the way to goodness, kindness and safety,
Sila's lamp of ethics shines,

causing the natural morality in the human heart to rise
to the cosmos and come back to serve all beings.

Larry Ward, untitled, water color, pen and ink, 2022.

RACE
Clouds Over the Moon

Somebody Stole My Face

"It's my face, man."
I tell you, somebody stole my face.
I can't seem to stop this river of regret.
Black face on the ground, black face in the cages.
Black face in chains, black face, no fun.

I tell you, somebody stole my face,
When I found it, it was dark like the night's elegant beauty.
When I found it, it was in a dreadful theater
called the White Man's Burden.
When I found it, it was already condemned to live
in a basket of lies.

I tell you, somebody stole my face, my precious face.
I hold it in my hands, catching tears of sorrow and joy.
I hold it with the kind hands of my ancestors.
I hold it turning into many faces, appearing
across time and space.

I hold it dancing with the cosmos.
In this face the door of eternity swung open.
I tell you, somebody stole my face.
But I have a secret for you, my friend.

Somebody stole your face too.
I know you've been searching for it.
It's in the time before time.
Embrace your wholeness.
Lift yourself and all the rest of us to higher ground.

And remember,
Every time you touch your face,
George Floyd can no longer have that joy.

It's a Pity

It's a pity

not to know
you are beautiful.

Not to know
you've been taught to hate.

Not to know
you have the key.

Not to know
that a gentle life has value.

Not to know
you are here to heal your ancestors.

Not to know
you are the earth's medicine.

Some Chimps Stole the Mic

Praising the doctrine of discovery day and night.

Perfuming the land with manifest destiny.

Now furious, ego's anger rises
as it discovers that it is not destined
to become the God it wished to be.

Because it was never intended for anyone to be that God.

Some chimps stole the mic.

Look At Us

Our racial suffering
is deep and wide.
A train wreck
of misery.

Never repaired.
Cycling
dangerous curves.
We are day and night scared.

Massive emergency.
Bodies on road and in ground.
Look at us, rubbernecking.
No urgency.

Gospel Sounds

Bones of our ancestors still dance
in the melody of stardust.

There, in the thick jungles of Costa Rica I was told
my mother passed
through the veil of no coming and no going.
I was heartbroken, going nowhere but sorrow, but sorrow.

The cry of an unknown bird cracked open the moment.
Ripe! Ripe! Ripe! The music of my roots rose up
from the earth to heal my soul.

A rainbow bridge appeared.
I climbed grief's holy mountain path
wet with the salt of healing tears.

Music lifted me up from the edge of grief's pit.
On the wings of sound I rode
with the mysteries of grace and peace.

Music's vibrations touch and quake where
the mind dares not.
Pain-healing sound picked up on the dusty road
of wounded souls.

Music lifted me up from the edge of grief's deep pit.
On the wings of sound I rode
with the mysteries of grace and peace in every moment.

Take up your rightful residence in your "Hale Manna."
Your spiritual house.
Come in, enter the clear light of sweet jazz.

Take your stand on the fearless dragon of compassion.
Ride the sacred waves of birth and death.
Let go of regret's gossamer threads
still attached to your heartbeat.

Now catch your precious breath.
Enter right now! Right now! Right now!
Music is a wild thing.
Music is a wild thing.
Music is a wild thing.

Contemplation on Black Lives Matter

I woke up this morning in a cauldron of fury and sadness.
You may not understand my anger
because it is filtered through your shame.
Shared fires of fury rage in all our bodies.

Tears of sadness burn.
Stop projecting fear on my darkness.
Place yourself in confinement.
Recognize your nervous breakdown.

Get some rest.
Try a little tenderness.
Feel something other than pride.
Taste the holy nectar of humility.

Debate broke out in thought.
Asked for centuries, *are non-whites human?*
No one asked, *are whites human?*
The sustainable injustice of American apartheid.

I don't want to live in your house.
I want to live in my house safely.
I don't want your job, I want my job opportunities.
I don't want your skin, I want mine unharmed.

Found in yard signs,
shouted in streets and villages on our planet,
black lives matter,
black lives have always mattered.

Africa is our mother.

Africa Before Africa

A toe jam of quantum particles
waves of mystery and madness
giving form to all humanity.

Grasslands and rain
rich earth rises expressing
herself in many forms.

The human genome
let loose for adaptation

changing our skin
to fit the climate,
the bush, the earth,
the rock, the animals.

Changing our language
so we can communicate
for survival, family rituals,
and dances
to calm our nerves
and minds.

We evolve through
the mystery
of time and space
emerging.

Not Lost

I am not lost, just painfully ignored.
I know this place
the shield of invisibility.
Irrelevant.
Yet hiding.
Replaceable.

The fog of loneliness within me,
envelopes my whole body and mind.
I realize I miss myself.

I miss you all,
wonders of life.
I cannot find holy ground.

What is to hold me up?
No space inside for me.
No room outside.
All others lost.

I'm just lost.
Needlessly unsafe.
I am already a wonder.

What is my path through?
Confusion's forest is thick.

But the path,
already in me,
reveals itself in every step,
every breath.

All Hail Sorrow

Sailing across oceans of suffering.
Sorrow is my home.

Emmett's sweet face now
destroyed by hate, jealousy,
ignorance. A memory capsule.
Destruction of black bodies.

I was seven years old with a broken heart.
My eyes flooded with tears,
I drowned in grief too large for me.
Scales of justice clouded truth.

Peace is possible in this life, justice too.
Don't ride the waves of hate.
Violence traumatizes our humanity.
In the ground now Emmett offers a prayer.

All Hail Sorrow.

An Incomplete Story

Such a beautiful
incomplete story:
America.

Made of dreams and suffering.
No escape.
Many elements that make us great.

Adapt America, let the frozen places in us melt.
Never without talent, land of fresh ideas,
make the impossible possible.

Identity trapped in cycle.
Belonging and othering.
Are we cursed?

Don't Get Too Dark

Don't get too dark
whatever you do
don't get too dark.

It is a curse
an affliction
one cannot hide.
Play it safe my friend
don't get too dark.

Unknown.
Frightening.
Alluring.
Death.
Dark wins in the end.

Eyes Opened

When my eyes opened this morning,
I knew who won the US 2024 election and why.
I say, if you wanted to build an all-white nation
you should not have brought my ancestors here.

Slaving fields of cotton and tobacco,
breaking backs laying railroad track,
fixing and raising children not our own,
tolerating and transcending cruelty and tears.

Our shared trauma, deep as an ocean.
A chasm of suffering haunts us all.
Our precious lives poured out seeking affirmation.

So troubled by the wounds of time
we are filled with the unspeakable.
How can we conquer?

First, know that we can.

Colonial Habits

We are still contending with 16th century habits.
Thought, language, perception and behaviors
like salmon swimming upstream to die,
conditioned so deeply we don't hardly recognize it
indicated by props of status, race, gender, classes of power.

I am a seeker of more than material wealth.
My nirvana is radical, profound and bone-trembling.
A mystery steeped in glory and suffering.
Claim your humanity.
Recognize your name is in love's net.

Playing hide and seek with its face,
cultivating the Nirvana mind,
the little boy from Cleveland had no idea
of blessings to come.

Ships of Perfume

The world has been perfumed by white supremacy.
A trail of blood and gold
holds suffering in conquest,
refuses to cross mercy's bridge.

Conditioned not to be together, we
stand now before a chasm of growth or death
out of alignment with our true humanity.
This is our reckoning.

Learning to raise each other up like flowers,
opening stories of our lives,
we recognize the good crossing mercy's bridge.

Our retribution is that we live with a tragic legacy,
a costly story that does not tame the beast within.
Being a human being is to tame that beast.
The wheel of America's racial karma is turning
if you have eyes to see.

Our racialized consciousness continues our tragic toxic tale.
Mixing rage and sadness and ancestors' blood
that is America's racial karma.
We still can witness this suffering.
If one of us gets sick, we are all infected;
if one of us gets well, we are all healed.

Troubles

We are in a trance.
Fixed in place or going backwards.
We are in trouble.
It is big—we don't know how big.
How deep is this trouble?
Enough to rattle sabers in the colonial mind.
Greed, hate, and ignorance.
All stunts we take for real.
The magician assumes we are children.

I Cried

I cried again in the early morning darkness.
I dared to see some kind of world news.
Wars within ourselves, wars between and among ourselves.

The worst kind of madness
is a madness that does not know it is mad,
a sickness that does not recognize itself as ill.

It breeds in deep disconnection
with the I, we, and the natural world.

The worst kind of madness pretends,
quite skillfully,
that it is not mad at all.

This virus of consciousness
is so deep
it can only be transformed
by going deeper into our true nature.

Do we not know
can we not recognize
can we not name
the madness we share?

The madness of threatening ourselves
with death constantly
and thinking that this defines a good society
is a mark of illness.

It is time for spiritual maturity to step up.
We are new consciousness to be witnessed
now in the community
beyond limiting constructs of gender, race, age, and class.

Join in with prose, poetry, plays, music, art, and dance
that carry us beyond the dualism of birth and death,
join in with the sincerity of pure hearts.

A new sanity is arising a little bit everywhere.
Hidden by the mists of ignorance,
the prison of unhealed trauma
and the addiction to the poisons of greed,
hate and ignorance born of fear.

When I Became Currency

When they came for me, I tried to contain my fear.
Heartbreak rattled my bones.
These bones longed for home but the dance of my ancestors
is still awake and alive,

sick in the bottom of a ship
becoming a dark currency.
Carried over the sea, sold and sold again, a commodity,
body of profit driven by greed, arrogance, and ignorance.

Cold and beleaguered in a new land,
I tried to forget such horror
but the looks and whispers even to this day remind me
I am a class of color created by a colonial mind
that was missing its self-worth.

I live now beyond such limiting constructs of mind.
I am free because I am not confused.
I am stardust awake.
I am the earth and sky embracing all.

I ride the wind with the eagle and the hawk.
I flow with the rivers into all oceans.
I touch the sun and am touched by the moonlight
like all beings.
I am Nature herself. Awake. Powerful. Resilient.
Generative.

I offer the love of all my ancestors to your ancestors
and the ancestors of all beings.
I offer my presence like rain falling
on the wise and the unwise,
the troubled and the untroubled,
the just and the unjust.

May wounds of time be healed.

American Purge

Settlers Mind
Forgetfulness
Genocide
Memories
History
Language
People
Swan song
White savior
Never was
Slippery slope
Protect others from your contagion
That's love
Heal bias
Transform

Colonial Mind's Backlash

Some people think white people
are the apex of human evolution.
They are not.
None of us are.
It must come as a fearful moment
of consciousness when one realizes
we are not through becoming
colonial mind's backlash.

Thinking

Wipe away my footprints from the scene of the crime.
Our thinking is the thinking of our ancestors.
Our thinking is the thinking of our cultural caves of up-
bringing.

Our thinking is the thinking of our conditioning.
We're not simply encapsulated egos.

This American Brexit will also fail because America
is made of non-American elements.

Governing by logic is not enough.
Governing by opinion is not enough.
Let's include governing by the heart.

I wish not to be blemished.

Frozen

To be frozen in fear can't be comfortable,
constant cold chilling your bones.
You hardly feel that you are alive.

Ears closed, eyes closing,
throat constricted, all symptoms
of being frozen. Now,
in this year, in this country,
in this culture, in this chaos.

If we could only find the sun.

Larry Ward, untitled, water color, 2022.

NATURE
Light in the Forest

January 1st

Leaves that fall
at night make
a softer sound
when they touch
the Earth.

Where do broken hearts
go in the middle
of life's windstorm?
I shall go to the
river of love
for my tears
to nourish
my heart.

Sit down and
wait patiently
for my river
of tears dammed
up by suppression
to survive.

Letting go of sadness,
falling like a leaf
in the still night.
I am happy and free
to greet the sun rise
of a new day,
a new year,
a new life.

Is a Caterpillar On My Back?

Is a caterpillar on my back?
I was told it was there.
A friend can see where I cannot.

Suffering Stops

Face of a deer in the window,
brown eyes looking back at my brown eyes, smiling.

The silence of the blue lake looking back
at the silver blue sky. Silence within.

All the while birds are enjoying their symphony
and mother earth's green leaves are wrapping us in
her compassion.

What a delightful surprise,
my heart is falling into the beauty of this spot.

Just then I hear the clock on the kitchen wall
Tick tock, tick tock, tick tock.

Just the other day, that sound meant time is running out.

But at this moment, it simply means
I can hear the sound of the kitchen clock ticking.

Tick tock, tick tock, tick tock.
Suffering stops.

I Am Present

I already lie in the green forest. Can you not see me there?
I am present in the movement of the trees
and the softness and hardness of the earth.
I ride on the wings of birds and speak
to fairies every night. What a wonderful rest
to be held by the Earth and unforgotten.

I already lie in the forest. Can you not see me there?
In the flutter of the chipmunks and the smiles
of the deer with their beautiful eyes, I am there too,
and at the sunrise and sunset, I say hello to you always.
When you walk on the precious Earth, remember you
are walking on me. I created in the galaxy of stars
bringing life to many beings. How can we not know each other?
We have the same mother and father.

I already lie in the forest. Can you not see me there?
The owls all night and the coyotes too
saying hello and goodbye every moment.
We too are saying goodbye and hello every moment.
How precious our moments are on this earth
in the midst of this mystery we smile
and cry in the unknown and yet known.

I already lie in the forest. Can you not see me there?
I am a raindrop falling on a leaf
nursing, all things. I am a leaf
at home in the forest singing
my song of regeneration.

I already lie in the forest. Can you not see me there?

Stars

I was numb until stars fell on my head.

I was lost in restlessness
until they held me in their magical arms.
I beheld myself as one of them,
finally shining in the dark.

My mind's clarity rides on the wings of hummingbirds,
and I smile.
I recognize the voices of prairie dogs and magpies
as my own.

I am here now and that's all,
entrusting myself to the awakening at hand.
Like the blessed mountains that surround us,
who know no fear.

What Nots

Recently
a memory of my grandmother
came to visit.

Sitting in her chair
with a shelf of what nots
behind her.

Small collectables of time
still shining.

Palms Up

A solitary leaf floats down,
landing on a bed of leaves.
Waiting. Palms facing the sky.

Not I

When the mirror no longer sees me smiling
I'm gone.
But the "not I" remains:
fire, water, earth, air, light, dark stars,
light galaxies, causes, conditions, mystery,
vivid memories, touches, voices, smiles,
faces of meaning, smells of delight.
All streams of mind, heartbreak too.

I am moved.
In every raindrop, in everything,
I look for you.
So we still can meet
In the silence of the moment.

Trees

I've been listening to trees
Redwoods, Pine, Oak.
Too many to name.

They worry and pray
over us
offering gratitude.

A message:
We do not love deeply enough
or wide enough.
This is the cause of
our madness.

Be Like the Rain

To be like the rain, falling on the just and the unjust
Such a desire lives in the heart of all Great Beings
like the rain watering seeds of goodness in every direction
to quench the fever of suffering in the hearts and
minds of all.

This holy embodiment rolls like thunder
opening hearts to the path of compassion
sometimes softly and sometimes loudly
to all who have ears to wake up, wake up. Wake up!

This presence in the world, like a torch
lighting up the dark and forgotten places in our minds.
To be awakened to our precious life and our precious planet
follow the torch and surrender.

Be like the rain falling without worry
because nothing less is worthy of our souls.

Larry Ward, Okunoin Cemetary, Mount Koya, Japan, mixed media, 2023.

ACKNOWLEDGEMENTS

I offer boundless gratitude to all the people, institutions, and beings who have contributed to this body of poetry. My wife, Peggy, encourages me to share my poetry at every teaching event, and she harvests all the poems I scribble on scraps of paper and envelopes. Grace Franklin transcribed poems that I offered at retreats in Ohio. Karen Hilsberg searched through years of journals and compiled a collection of my poems into a manuscript. Karen and Grace worked together to collect poems from many streams. Without their work, this book would not exist.

Elizabeth Chambers helped craft this collection through her tremendous support and talent in design, organization, and editing. Thanks to the support of Annie and Paul Mahon we had the guidance of Martha Bullen throughout the entire publishing process—her knowledge and wisdom were invaluable. The open-hearted generosity of Leslie Brunker provided funds for Erik Fuhrer, an experienced editor from Yellow Bird Editors.

Thanks to the many readers who offered feedback, including Elli Weisbaum and her students at the University of Toronto, Annie Mahon, Matt Dorma, Mona Abutaleb, Celeste Ferrson, and the Lotus Institute community. The Plum Village sangha and The Mindfulness Bell have been the wind beneath my feet.

I am grateful for our friends on the path, including Reverend Angel, Lama Rod, Pamela Ayo Yetunde, Gaylon Ferguson, Elli Weisbaum, Rima Vesely-Flad,

Kaira Jewel Lingo, Ruth King, Jan Willis, Krista Tippett, Rob Work, Sister Peace, Brett Cook, Valerie Brown, Jean Houston, Kazu Haga, Reggie Hubbard, Rhonda Magee, Zenju Earthlyn Manuel, Kamilah Majied, and Reverend Beth Johnson.

I am grateful for the many communities who contributed to these poems through their presence and practice, including William Edelglass and The Barre Center for Buddhist Studies, Diana Parra Perez and the University of Richmond, Teijo and Great Tree Zen Women's Temple, Princeton University, the bell hooks gathering at Harvard University, the African American Dharma Teachers, the Bess Family, Ivan Mayerhofer and Davidson College, Emory University, Pat Webb and Maurice Hoover, Prairie Wind Sangha in Oklahoma City, Grace Franklin and the Blue Heron Sangha in Columbus, Ohio, Mat Sherman and Margit Sereny, Viviane Ephraimson-Abt and Paul McClure, Compassionate Heart Sangha and the Colorado Community of Mindful Living, Cambridge Insight Meditation Center, Gift, Grandfather, and our Order of Interbeing friends in Thailand, Tetsu and Hisako Koizumi, Laura and Monica Alvarado, Jorge Hirsch, Norma Inez of the Mexico City Sangha, the Kwan Um Zen Sangha, Sosun and Clouds in Water, His Lai Temple, Ben Connelly and Ted O'Toole and the Minnesota Zen Center, Claremont School of Theology, The University of the West, Fo Guan

Shan Temple, Hsi Lai Temple, Great Vow Monastery, and Duncan Williams and May We Gather.

I am grateful for the prayers and quiet support of Kate Cummings, John and Cindy West, Joan and Andre Watts, Steve and Andrea Hopke, Reverend Anne Clement, Susan Glogovac, Diane Little Eagle, Elaine Miller-Karas, Brad Wiscons, Lin Colavin, Beth Benjamin, Joe Reilly, Father Thomas Keating, Mary Zinkin, Ricky and Judi Nakatomi, Angeles Arrien, Gary and Helena Hill, Father Adam Bucko, and the Temples of Kyoto.

I send mighty prayers of thanksgiving to the poets and writers who helped me find my writer's voice, including James Baldwin, bell hooks, Rainer Maria Rilke, Nikki Giovanni, Phillis Wheatley, D. H. Lawrence, Langston Hughes, Emily Dickinson, Stephen Crane, Robert Bly, Rumi, Kabir, Pablo Neruda, and Nikos Kazantzakis.

To my friend and teacher, Zen Master poet Thich Nhat Hanh: I see you everywhere. You are my breath. To Reverend Joseph Matthew, founder of my first religious order, I am grateful for your courage and inspiration.

And, of course, where would I be without the love and celebration of life freely given by Reggae, Charlie, and Tashi?

ABOUT THE AUTHOR

Larry Ward, PhD, is a poet, writer, spiritual teacher, and co-founder of The Lotus Institute. He is the acclaimed author of *America's Racial Karma: An Invitation to Heal*, and co-author of *Love's Garden: A Guide for Mindful Relationships*.

An ordained Christian minister and a senior Dharma teacher in Buddhist Zen Master Thich Nhat Hanh's Plum Village tradition, he holds a PhD in Religious Studies with an emphasis on Buddhism and the neuroscience of meditation.

As a teacher, Larry interweaves insights with personal stories and resounding clarity that express his dharma name, True Great Sound. Throughout his years of teaching, he has written poetry that assists in delivering and clarifying his messages to share in his talks. His new book, *Morning Night: Poems on Spirit, Race, and Nature* is a compilation of these poems.

Larry enjoys British mysteries, studying Buddhist sutras, and spending time with his wife, Peggy, and dog, Tashi, at their home in Rhode Island. His current passion is learning the stories and names of the many birds and plants in his backyard. His favorite mindfulness activity is the practice of open awareness from a chair on his back patio.

To learn more or contact Larry, visit www.thelotusinstitute.org.